THE GERMAN AMBASSADOR'S RESIDENCE

in London

THE GERMAN AMBASSADOR'S RESIDENCE

in London

By Regine Aldington

With photographs by
Fritz Graf von der Schulenburg and Marianne Majerus

John Adamson
Cambridge

Support for the publication of this book was provided by Deutsche Bank AG.

Published by John Adamson,
            90 Hertford Street,
            Cambridge CB4 3AQ, England

First published 1993 (0 9524322 0 X)
Second edition 2003 (0 9524322 1 8)

Edited by Catherine Mason
Designed by Christine Jones, Design 4 Science Ltd
Printed by Balding + Mansell, Norwich on Job Parilux Matt Cream 135 gsm
This paper supplied by Scheufelen Premium Papers, T. 01737 234530

Frontispiece: a full-length state portrait of George IV after Thomas Lawrence, above a gilded late 19th-century ottoman

CONTENTS

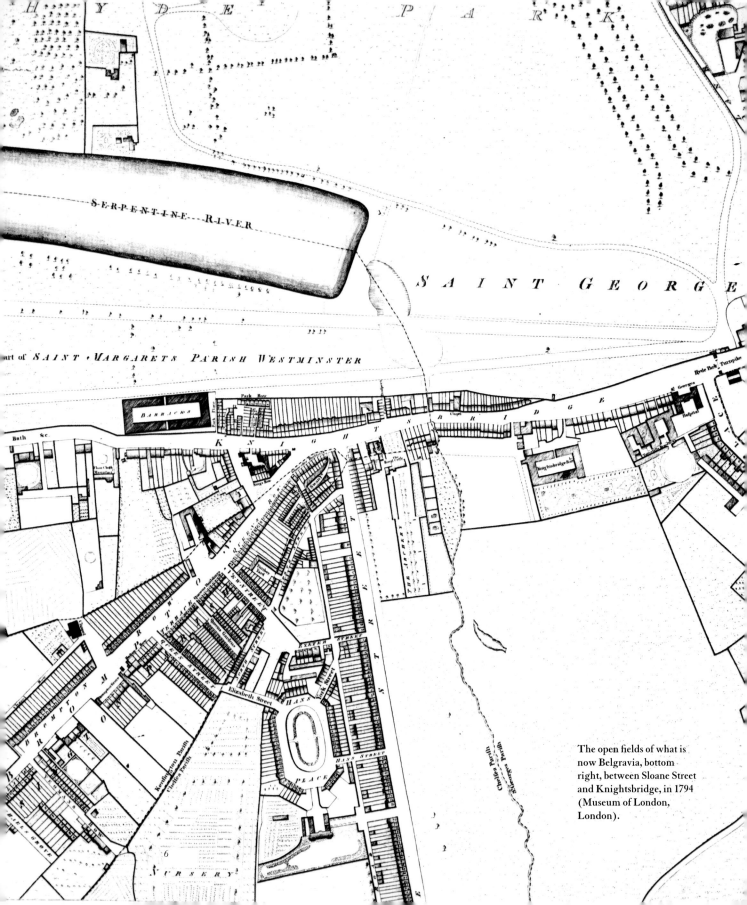

The open fields of what is now Belgravia, bottom right, between Sloane Street and Knightsbridge, in 1794 (Museum of London, London).

6

HISTORICAL BACKGROUND

The establishment of the German Embassy at 21–23 Belgrave Square is a rather recent episode in a long and eventful history of German diplomatic missions to Great Britain. It is only since the unification of East and West Germany in 1990 that the embassy has represented the whole of Germany. Until then the German Democratic Republic had its own foreign mission, located nearby at 34 Belgrave Square (first as a consulate from 1967 to 1973 and then as an embassy from 1973 to 1990).

While still in the process of formation and consolidation after World War II, the young Federal Republic of Germany sent Dr. Hans Schlange-Schöningen as its first consul general to London in 1950. The temporary quarters of the consulate were at 4–6 Rutland Gate, until a 99-year lease was drawn up between the Duke of Westminster and the German representative for the use of 21–23 Belgrave Square.

It took nearly three years to convert the three adjacent houses at that address into one. By the time the rooms were ready to move into, in 1955, the consulate had been restored to the status of embassy and Hans von Herwarth had succeeded Dr. Schlange-Schöningen. In 1977 the residence was enlarged by a modern office block at the back, overlooking Chesham Place. Two major refurbishments have taken place since, in 1989–91 and in 1998, when the reception rooms were newly decorated by Alec Cobbe and David Mees.

Until the outbreak of World War II, the German diplomatic mission had its seat at 9 Carlton House Terrace. Originally leased on behalf of the Prussian Legation in 1849, this mission had been only one of a dozen or so legations from individual German states and cities. Following the foundation of the German Reich in 1871, the Prussian Legation became the

prima inter pares as the German Imperial Embassy. It was only with the end of the First World War and the collapse of imperial Germany that these semi-sovereign German states gave up their own separate foreign missions. Only the Carlton House Terrace mission was to remain, serving first as residence for the representatives of the Weimar Republic and then for those of the Third Reich.

In 1936–37 the embassy was enlarged by the addition of the house next door at no. 8. The lease for this residence expired in 1948 and neither party had the wish or the need to seek to renew it. At that time Germany did not have any diplomatic missions as such in any country. The Federal Republic of Germany was founded in May 1949 and was recognized from the outset by Great Britain. From its temporary location the consulate's search for new and more spacious premises began, and in 1953 the contract for the three adjacent Belgrave Square houses was completed. The German Democratic Republic, however, which was founded in October of the same year, was only granted diplomatic recognition by Great Britain in 1973. Nevertheless in 1970 the GDR opened a trade mission without diplomatic status in London. The mission was headed by Dr. Dieter Butters, and it found an equally convenient location almost next door at 34 Belgrave Square. When diplomatic recognition was granted in 1973, Karl Heinz Kern, the chargé d'affaires—and from January 1974 ambassador extraordinary and plenipotentiary—was sent to London, where he took up residence at no. 34. With the arrival of German unification the last GDR ambassador, Dr. Jochen Mitdank, was called back in June 1990. On 3 October 1990 the then ambassador of the Federal Republic, Dr. Hermann von Richthofen, became the first ambassador for the united Germany. The premises of no. 34 were kept as offices.

The history of the origins of the former Prussian and the current residences are both, albeit in different ways, closely connected with King George IV (Prince Regent from 1811 and King from 1820 to 1830). When he was Prince of Wales his father had given him Carlton House to use as his London residence. From 1783 onwards, he was endlessly converting, renovating and enlarging the place, until it became a magnificent ensemble. When he succeeded to the throne he lost all interest in Carlton House, and threw himself into the task of beautifying what was then still called Buckingham House. Carlton House was finally demolished, although many of its architectural elements were salvaged to be used in Windsor Castle, Buckingham Palace, the Brighton Pavilion and, in the case of the spectacular columns, for the portico of the National Gallery.

This extensive and now vacant site provided a wonderful opportunity for John Nash, the King's favourite architect. Despite being engaged in the King's sumptuous refurbishment plans for Buckingham Palace, he also found the time between 1827 and 1832 to design and build the two prestigious rows of townhouses forming Carlton House Terrace. Soon after their completion the Prussian Legation moved in.

In the 1830s the area to the west and south-west of Buckingham Palace was still barely developed. What we know as Belgravia today was then little more than swampy fields, traversed by the Westbourne, a small stream, ensuring a constant and plentiful population of ducks. It became a favourite place for socializing and shooting fowl. Since the Middle Ages this tract of land had been known as "The Five Fields", after the ancient footpaths which criss-crossed and effectively partitioned the land.

The King's decision to take Buckingham House as his residence had the immediate and inevitable effect of attracting speculators to the scene. Not only was there a keen interest in areas conveniently close to the Palace and to Westminster, but the population of London in general grew so rapidly that new housing developments became a pressing necessity. Even though London was already one of the largest cities in Europe, its population more than doubled between 1800 and 1840 (from roughly 1 million to 2.2 for greater London). After almost thirty years of military dispute with France—which culminated in the Continental Blockade—England was beginning to recover economically after the turning point of the Battle of Waterloo in 1815.

John Nash (1752–1835), John Soane (1753–1837) and the slightly younger Robert Smirke (1781–1867), together with their pupils, exercised between them the greatest influence on the architectural development of the time. During the later Regency period and under George IV's reign, the whole of London could be described as one huge building site. Among the "Metropolitan Improvements" [1] of this period were Regent Street and the buildings facing Regent's Park, the redesigning of Hyde Park and St. James's Park, as well as the planning and laying out of what became Battersea Park. The reconstruction of Whitehall and Westminster as we know them today also occurred at this time, as did the construction of the British Museum and the National Gallery.

By forcing the large pillars and columns left over from dismantling Carlton House onto the state's new museum project of a National Gallery, the King was hoping to strike a deal with a government already exasperated at having to foot the bills for his building extravagances. With this generous gift to the nation, George IV was hoping for positive reactions to further demands for cash. As the columns only arrived when the new museum project was well under way, their subsequent incorporation resulted in the rather odd proportions of the façade.

The Royal Mint, the old General Post Office (demolished in 1912) and the Bank of England also

Thomas Cubitt
(1788–1855), the
great building
entrepreneur, by
an unknown artist
(National Portrait
Gallery, London).

originate from this period of building mania. Countless churches and theatres such as Drury Lane, Haymarket and Covent Garden, as well as gentlemen's clubs including the Travellers' and the Athenaeum, shot up in every possible nook and cranny. New bridges linked the areas north and south of the river, and new docks enlarged the port installations, testifying to Britannia's determination to rule the waves.

Yet even though London was the city of Royal Residence, with patron kings who defined the style and fashion, it was more genuinely a metropolis of merchants and traders than a city marked by court culture. After the downfall of Napoleon, England considered herself the saviour of Europe and a new sphere of influence, with London at the very centre. This mood of national pride and exertion was further reflected in the free use of a variety of architectural styles, such as Egyptian, Chinese, Pompeiian, Hindu, Greek or Gothic; extravagances characterized by the Royal Pavilion in Brighton, designed by Humphrey Repton and John Nash for the Prince Regent. This medley of styles and directions was subsequently subdued by the "pragmatic aesthetic" of Nash, and by Soane's "sobriety",[2] into the nineteenth-century classicism which still defines so much of central London today.

When general interest in the "Five Fields" became apparent, the ingenious entrepreneur Thomas Cubitt (1788–1855) seized the opportunity. He had begun his career as a simple carpenter and steadily worked his way up through the 1820s to the 1840s, until he had become the country's largest building contractor. Cubitt secured the building rights for the "Five Fields" from the 2nd Earl Grosvenor, whose descendant later was created the 1st Duke of Westminster in 1874. The area, known as Belgravia, was soon to become the shining jewel in the crown of the Duke of Westminster's estate— which it still is today.

In order to finance the project, Cubitt formed a syndicate, among the main financiers of which were Alexander Prevost and the banker Robert Smith, the 1st Baron Carrington. Subsequently the Swiss banker brothers George and William Haldimand acquired the leasehold on thirty of the houses in Belgrave Square and joined the syndicate. William was later to become the director of the Bank of England. By sheer coincidence, one of the financiers, Alexander Prevost, lived in no. 22, now part of the German Embassy, whereas William Haldimand occupied no. 18, now the Austrian Embassy, and his brother George no. 31.

From the very beginning Belgravia had been planned to rival Mayfair, which also belonged to the Grosvenor Estate. The project's resounding success proved the speculators right. This time Cubitt did not fulfil the function of architect as he had done in many of his other projects. His contribution to Belgravia was the master plan. After the Grosvenor Estate surveyors had submitted a general block plan for the partitioning of the area, Cubitt set to work on the details of the layout of the streets and the square, the service accommodation in the shape of mews and stables, as well as the entire infrastructure, and finally the supervision of the project. It is very likely that Grosvenor's personal architect, Thomas Cundy the younger, was also consulted on these general matters. Very expediently, Cubitt found his building materials on the site of the intended square. The excavations produced a large supply of clay, which was ideal for baking bricks on the spot. To fill up the square again he used the earth and gravel from the St. Katherine's Dock excavations, which he had recently completed. The area did not, however, reach its former level, which accounts for the slight rise of the ground from Belgrave Square towards Hyde Park Corner. This was another enterprise where William Haldimand and Cubitt had mutual interests insofar as Haldimand was a director of the St. Katherine's Dock.

Cubitt and the Haldimand brothers, who dominated the syndicate, took charge of engaging an architect for their project. The choice fell upon the young and fairly inexperienced George Basevi (1794–1845).[3] He had two major advantages: he was a pupil of John Soane and a distant relative of Disraeli. This choice of an unknown young man must have come as a surprise to many interested architects, but may be explained by Basevi's previous activities. Following the end of his studies in 1816 he had travelled extensively through Greece and Italy for three years. Upon his return he soon received his first commission. This was a project for David Ricardo, a well-known banker, Member of Parliament and political economist. In keeping with the example set by the King, Ricardo wanted his country estate, Gatcombe Park in Gloucestershire, to be rebuilt and enlarged. Today Gatcombe Park is owned by H.R.H. the Princess Royal. It is not quite clear how the next contract—between Basevi and the Haldimand syndicate—came about; it may have been through the latter's City connections via Ricardo, or political connections through the Disraeli family, or through intervention from Cubitt who seems to have promoted the young architect's talent. In any event, Basevi received his first independent commission from William Haldimand to design and build him a country house: Ashgrove in Kent. The result must have been very much to Haldimand's satisfaction, as Basevi was eventually entrusted with the new project of Belgrave Square.

Initially only the north and east sides of the square were erected and then, as their success became apparent, the south and west elevations followed suit. It is on the square's western side where the residence and embassy are situated. The three detached corner buildings were individually designed shortly afterwards by other architects.[4]

The process was such that the architect provided the drawings for the outer shell of the buildings, chiefly the front elevation. The client then chose the layout of the rooms and even determined, to some extent, the depth of the house and, where appropriate, the shape of the mews. This accounts for the distinct variations in back yards and almost total disregard for the rear elevations.

The resounding success of this large project established Basevi's reputation and set him on the road to a brilliant career. His next projects were on Pelham Place and Crescent, Egerton Crescent, Walton Place and Thurloe Square. Between 1853 and 1843–4, he and Smirke re-built the old Carlton Club on Pall Mall, of which Benjamin Disraeli had become a member in 1836. He continued the club tradition and built the Conservative Club at 74 St. James's Street.

In 1833 Basevi and other architects had been invited to submit a blueprint for the new House of Commons. Though Basevi was not to win that commission, he did win the architectural contest to design the Fitzwilliam Museum in Cambridge. If there had been any further need to secure his reputation, this prestigious task made him widely and firmly known as a man of great ability and taste, and strengthened his claim to be acknowledged as one of the leading architects of his day. Sadly, his career came to an untimely end during an inspection visit to Ely. He had come to supervise some renovation work on the Cathedral when he fell off a scaffold.

In the early nineteenth century it was expected that a good architect should have a wide repertoire of styles at his disposal. According to the requirements of the client, Basevi could as easily design a Gothic church or houses in the Tudor style, such as, for example, his almshouses. Yet his classicism predominated not least owing to the influence of his teacher, Sir John Soane, although the example of Nash and the inspiration he derived from his first-hand studies of the classic originals in Greece and Italy must not be underestimated.

In the design for Belgrave Square he employed a rather moderate classic repertoire. Each of the four sides of the square consists of eleven or twelve houses, and each side is designed as an entity. Even if each house's façade may differ slightly from its neighbour, each of the four terraces is dealt with as a

A marble bust of
George Basevi
(1794–1845),
architect of
Belgrave Square
(Fitzwilliam
Museum,
Cambridge).

whole. Taking the western side as an example, all eleven houses are combined into one large front, resembling a stretched version of a classical *palais* with a protruding central building (no. 18, the Austrian Embassy) and two side blocks, accentuating and framing the terrace. Both central and corner buildings are more elaborately decorated with pilasters and columns, thus also taking into account the lively, three-dimensional effects of light and shade. The central building is made up of five vertical axes, counterbalancing the corner buildings (one of them being no. 22, part of the German Embassy) with three axes each. Not only the volume but also the degree of encrustation intensifies towards the centre. What is introduced at the corners as a bas-relief of the great classical order of Corinthian pilasters is repeated and enhanced in the central block, where each of the five axes is framed by mighty pilasters and full-sized columns, standing proud of the façade. This magnificent architectural decoration unites the two main floors into one vertical entity. Key windows of the *piano nobile* and upper floors are crowned by triangular pediments which again enhance the vertical line of the decoration, as do the vases set atop each lesene. Similar vases are found at attic level on either side of the central block. In comparison with the other floors this level is far more modestly adorned. Here these vases only top every third pier, where they serve to hide the firewalls. As a final flourish the pedimented central building (no. 18) is crowned by a coat-of-arms, borne by nymphs.

The impact of all these features can best be seen from a certain distance. When coming closer to the building the dominant feature increasingly becomes the identical portals at ground-floor level, standing out with their columns and protruding balconies at first-floor level. However, the vertical focal points at the centre and the ends are of vital importance to relieve the relative monotony of so wide a terrace. With only three storeys plus an additional attic in height against 35 paratactic axes in width, the sheer emphasis of the volume lies clearly in the horizontal. Therefore any further accentuation of horizontal features has been reduced to the mere requirements of the classical canon and applied sparingly. The rustication of the ground floor is plain and moderate; a rather simple and unobtrusive cornice spans the entire façade just below the window region of the second floor. This cornice is laid behind the columns and pilasters so as to give visual priority to their vertical impact. To separate the main floors from the attic Basevi made use of a dentil entablature such as he had seen on temples in Greece. The gabled roofs of the houses round the square are not visible from the street, as they are hidden by the superstructure of the attics.

Not much can be seen today of the original interior layout of rooms. Contrary to the continental custom, it was usual for buildings in London to be designed with a vertical rather than horizontal use of space. Much precious room was thus lost to allow for the numerous flights of stairs that were needed for access to all floors.

This vertical orientation of buildings also meant that large, generous suites of rooms after the French fashion did not exist.

The preservation of London's historical architectural styles and the interior reconstruction of these buildings were not due to any general aesthetic sense of duty on the part of the owners. The city's buildings were subject to constant and regular change; a turmoil which was closely related to the interests and organization of ownership. People generally built their houses on leased land. Thus every alteration and improvement during the span of a 99-year lease became the property of the landlord once that lease was up. It is not surprising that this policy did little to encourage "building for posterity". Only rather recently—with increasing awareness by the public of its national heritage—has the preservation of such old buildings been given greater priority. Considering the rapid changes in architectural styles in the preceding centuries, a

Victorian walking through the city today might be surprised to find that much of "his" London has hardly changed over the past 100 years.

The houses of 21–23 Belgrave Square were joined together in 1953, with the aim of creating a harmonious design to unite all three interiors. The structure was changed to create space for a large communal entrance hall and an open staircase leading up to the *piano nobile*. Galleries line the walls, to decorative and practical effect. A stunning new addition is the crowning glass dome, which allows sunlight to enter an otherwise relatively dark area and provides a focus for the visitor's gaze. Another consequence of combining the three buildings was that a suite of generous, linking rooms for entertaining could be created on the first floor.

The first thorough renovation took place between 1989 and 1991. The emphasis was then more on the interior decoration than on the structure of the building. Another re-decoration took place in 1998, this time to introduce a stunning colour scheme to the hitherto white and cream walls, cornices and ceilings of the main reception rooms. Today the visitor to the embassy finds a harmonious ensemble, which provides a stylish and elegant setting for social events of every kind.

Notes
1. *Metropolitan Improvements or: London in the 18th Century* (1827) by Thomas Hosmer Shepherd (drawings and prints) and James Elmes (text). A virtually complete documentation of the architectural happenings in the first quarter of the 19th century.
2. *Metropole London*, exhibition catalogue, Essen 1992, p. 70.
3. Colvin 1978, pp. 93–95.
4. South-east corner (no. 37): *Seaford House,* by Philip Hardwich for Lord Sefton; south-west corner (no. 24): Henry E. Kendell for Thomas Read Kemp; north-west corner (no. 12): Sir Robert Smirke for Lord Brownlow.

The residence of the
German Ambassador,
21–23 Belgrave Square.

THE ROOMS

A late 19th-century gilt mounted German mahogany mirror (opposite).

When the first post-war West German representative was ready to take up office in 1953, the rooms of the embassy needed to be decorated and furnished.

The first piece of furniture to be acquired for this purpose was the desk for the Ambassador's office. Its value is mainly sentimental and historical, as this was the desk from the office of Prince Lichnowsky, Germany's last Imperial Ambassador to the Court of St. James. It was there that he made the last desperate efforts to avert the looming danger of war in the last days of August 1914. His exertions, as the world well knows, came to naught, and the First World War began its destructive course.

Most of the furnishings have found their way to 21–23 Belgrave Square from government depots in Bonn. Other pieces came, and still do come, from private lenders such as the House of Hanover, and from German museums. The large variety of lenders accounts for an eclectic mingling of styles, which together form a harmonious ensemble. Beyond that, many of the pieces have, in different ways, connections to the history of the place, its purpose and its occupants.

Furniture and porcelain, paintings, tapestries, carpets, sculptures and other decorative objects were brought together and distributed throughout the various rooms. Although many of the items are museum pieces, the overall effect is not at all that of the somewhat fusty and unlived-in atmosphere of a museum which one might expect. The way in which the objects are grouped together, seemingly accidentally and with a lightness of touch, displays the charm of a collection which has been accumulated over time, even though the individual pieces cannot always claim to be of equal artistic value.

It is not by chance that this virtual tour through the embassy should begin with a large state portrait of King George IV, from the studio of Thomas Lawrence (see frontispiece). It was this king who influenced the city's architecture to a great extent in the early nineteenth century and shaped much of London as we know it today, and as we have seen, it was during his reign that the buildings of Carlton House Terrace and Belgrave Square were erected. Both addresses were later to play an important role in the history of the German embassies in London. Though somewhat later in style, the German asymmetrically curved, carved and heavily gilded ottoman beneath his portrait breathes the same, still unshakable self-confidence, ostentation even, of an intact and prosperous society. The origin of this exquisite piece is not certain, but it was probably made in Berlin. Appreciation of this nineteenth-century Neo-Baroque style has only recently begun to pick up.

What would a German embassy be without a mention or two of Frederick the Great, or of Bismarck, for that matter? Sure enough, the embassy in London boasts a fine equestrian statue of Frederick the Great. It is a contemporary scaled-down replica of the full-size monument by Christian Daniel Rauch (1777–1857) in the middle of Unter den Linden in Berlin, and portrays the King as though he were just returning from a morning's trot in the Tiergarten outside the Brandenburg Gate. The statue was commissioned and executed after the King's death (1786) and was only unveiled in 1851, by which time the King had truly become a legend. Rauch's work was an immediate success and a large number of scale models flooded the market in its wake. With a gap of more than half a century between Frederick's death and the completion of this memorial, the King can hardly be held accountable for the iconography of the friezes. The rows of men around the plinth, on foot and on

A scale bronze replica of Christian Daniel Rauch's statue of Frederick the Great.

horseback, gave immediate grounds for the Berliners to exercise their trenchant wit: flanked by the four most distinguished generals on horseback on each corner, three of the sides are equally occupied by war heroes and eminent civic dignitaries. However the short fourth side, at the back and beneath the horse's tail, was chosen for the intellectuals: philosophers, musicians and writers. One wonders whether his military achievements, for which he gained the epithet "Great" really meant so much more to a king who played his flute every day and liked to sign his more private letters as "Fédéric le philosophe".

There is also reference to—and reverence for—a more recent chapter in German history: a bronze plaque and two photographs commemorate the lives of members of the German Embassy in London who joined the Resistance against Hitler during World War II. Councillor Albrecht Graf Bernstorff

and the Legation Secretary Eduard Brücklmeier were executed in Berlin in 1944, and the same fate befell the Attaché Herbert Mumm von Schwarzenstein in 1945, after their involvement in the plot had been uncovered. Supported by British friends, they had been trying to use their London outpost to liaise with the British Government in their desperate attempt to overthrow Hitler.

The warm and stunning yellow-ochre *faux* marble wall décor of the outer hall creates a sense of welcome and generosity. The room is almost bare but for a few selected items, such as a large north German writing cabinet from the middle of the eighteenth century. Its dark and shimmering walnut front extends from the two cupboard doors to the double-domed moulded cornice, culminating in plumed crestings on top of the two domes, the plumes being reminiscent of the Prince of Wales's feathers. Facing the windows there is a lively, large

Flemish Gobelin, the first of a valuable collection of tapestries to be seen scattered around the embassy. This particular one originates from Brussels, where it was made in the mid sixteenth century. Its theme, as the inscription on its lower border confirms, is from the Old Testament:

Van Davit en Abigail
1. Samvel Cap 25.

This episode from the Book of Samuel was a highly popular subject for wall hangings in dining rooms, as the scene allowed for a sumptuous presentation of any type of food. The Bible tells of 200 loaves of bread, 2 jugs of wine, 5 roasted sheep, 5 bushels of flour, 100 clusters of raisins and 200 fig cakes. These were the presents which Nabal's wife Abigail brought to David in order to appease him, after he had been offended by her husband. Her offerings were not in vain; the war and destruction threatening her people were averted. During the Renaissance the portrayal of richly laden tables and opulent meals was one of the favourite themes. Not only did such presentations prepare men's minds and appetites for the joys of a festive meal, they also served to display the host's wealth and bounty and, of course, provided a suitably edifying setting for the guests.

What form of moralizing could have been more enjoyable than this? And what more suitable subject for a festive gathering, with the spectators almost drawn into participating at the banquet? All the little didactic hints of the biblical story were of course easy to decipher for the God-fearing and educated audiences of the time.

Two classical Roman-style busts add a serene and heroic accent to this outer hall. On high marble pillars raised to eye-height is a bronze of Lucius Junius Brutus, his shoulders draped with a toga of red marble. The second is a bust of the Emperor Augustus, his head fashioned in white marble, the breast-plate in dark yellow marble. They are from the late eighteenth century, which was the heyday of the Grand Tours, when every educated gentleman had to visit the continent, and particularly Rome, then regarded as one of the cradles of civilization. The fashion was either to bring back genuine antiques or to have sculptures made to resemble those antiques, and these two Roman heroes are from that period. Many of the great English country houses still contain substantial collections of these travel memorabilia; a great number of similar Roman busts can be seen at Wilton House.

Lucius Junius Brutus. A late 18th-century bronze bust adorned with red marble.

The Emperor Augustus. A late 18th-century white and yellow marble bust.

INNER HALL

The most notable object in the spacious adjacent inner hall is an oil painting by the Munich artist Max Emanuel Ainmiller (1807–70). Painted in 1851, it depicts the inner choir of Westminster Abbey, whose grandeur must have captivated him on a visit to London. Shortly afterwards he was entrusted with the prestigious commission of designing three stained-glass windows for St. Paul's Cathedral.

Munich stained glass was highly regarded at the time. Ainmiller's London patrons, who put him forward for the St. Paul project, must have been favourably impressed by his artistic achievements in this respect: he had already proved his ability as a glass painter in the medieval cathedrals of Speyer, Regensburg and Cologne, and had travelled extensively in Italy where he had met and subsequently worked with Moritz von Schwind and Julius Schnorr von Carolsfeld. To a certain extent it was through their influence that a new and deeply felt world of religious art was opened up to him; a world of monumental tales, myths and fantasy. This was an international artistic phenomenon, which in England culminated in the Pre-Raphaelite movement. Ainmiller's choice of depicting an intact and unspoiled Gothic section of the cathedral is typical of the enthusiasm of this group of artists for what they saw as the purity of the High Middle Ages. In keeping with this sentiment he populated his canvas with figures in medieval costume.

Together with Schnorr, who drew the original sketches, Ainmiller also created three windows for the choir of St. Paul's. Ironically, they were among the windows destroyed in an air raid in World War II.

Underneath this picture is a serpentine front *bombé* commode, an unusual example of north German or possibly Dutch late Baroque style; some features, however, point more to the nineteenth century, using the style and technique of the later eighteenth. The use of various types of wood from the Caribbean, and above all the style of inlay, are quite rare. The entire commode is inlaid with diagonal bands of equal width. The almost austere, diamond-shaped pattern, identical on the front and the sides of this piece of furniture, provides an interesting contrast to the generous, softly curving contour of all three sides. The curves meet at the corners to form sharp serpentine contours.

The armchairs on either side of the commode are part of a group of Baroque *fauteuils*, which are probably the most valuable armchairs in the building. They are partly made from beech, partly walnut. Walnut was a great favourite during the German Baroque because of its shimmering reddish-brown hue and relatively soft grain, which

Max Emanuel Ainmiller's Inner Choir of Westminster Abbey (1851), above an unusual German commode, probably a 19th-century copy of a late Baroque type (opposite).

Inner hall: a late 17th-century refectory table. To the right a marble bust of Frederick the Great by Rauch, early 19th century.

lent itself well to carving yet was also hard-wearing. The delicacy of the decorative carving, the contours of the chairs as well as their height and depth reveal their mid eighteenth-century origin.

Next to the connecting doors hangs a splendid late Baroque mirror. The glass is surrounded by a carved wooden frame, which rises in a crest of pierced and foliated carving, incorporating a small, glass-covered painted cartouche of the god Pan bound to a tree. This type of mirror is typical of northern Italy in the late eighteenth century.

The furnishing of the inner hall is completed by a long refectory table (2.65 x 0.64 metres [c. 8 ft. 8 in. x 2 ft. 1 in.]), dating from the late seventeenth century. The basic functional design of such tables remained relatively unvaried over many centuries. Determining a date for such a table would be difficult, were it not for the design of its supports: the four heavy, turned legs with their stretchers quite close to the ground indicate the table's date fairly accurately. A witness to the gatherings of many generations of monks, it now serves to display two dinandery plates of embossed brass. They owe their unusual name to their place of origin: Dinant in Belgium, where embossed copper and brass plates, salvers and vessels were made from as far back as the fifteenth century. Their popularity abroad soon led to the Dinant name being employed as a trademark. The consequence of this popularity was that dinandery production and export guaranteed work for many generations of artists from the early fifteenth up to the nineteenth century. Careful not to spoil the established brand name by introducing new products, the technique and designs of the plates remained unaltered throughout. Since the decorative motives were all religious and heraldic they could always count on a safe market.

By the side of the stairs leading to the first floor reception rooms there is another effigy of Frederick the Great, also from the workshop of Christian Daniel Rauch. Here there is no allusion to his martial achievements or to the public man. The artist portrays an ageing man, his hair untied, no tricorn hat, his head straight, his expression that of a serene yet pensive man, marked by the burden of his duties, yet unflinching in the face of challenge. The bust of this statesman and philosopher in exquisite white marble conveys an impression of great simplicity—"Prussian Simplicity"—which in later times was often to be misunderstood and mistaken for lack of imagination and blind obedience. Instead of military attire, Frederick is clothed in a classic, late Baroque type of drapery. The only token of his dignity is the medal of the highest Prussian order, the Black Eagle, founded by his grandfather Frederick, the first King of Prussia, on the eve of his coronation in January 1701. Its motto "Suum Cuique" may, in its translation: "each to the best of his ability", also be interpreted as the King's anti-Machiavellian striving for tolerance.

Frederick the Great. An early 19th-century bust of white marble, attributed to Christian Daniel Rauch.

fur, jewellery and such—that alone would have been nothing new—but he even had the formats of his canvases standardized for easier processing. Each canvas measured 39 by 49 inches (99 x 124 cm). This standard became so famous that people even spoke of the "Kit-Cat format" in reference to these portraits. Today most of his thirty-two Kit-Cat portraits are at the National Portrait Gallery, London.

The three men portrayed by Kneller are: General Carpenter, a leading military figure in the decisive English victory over the Jacobites in the Uprising of 1715, when Scottish supporters of the Stuarts had attempted to establish their claim to the English throne; William Pulteney, a leading Whig politician of the opposition against Sir Robert Walpole, Britain's first Prime Minister, and lastly, James O'Hara, Lord Tyrawley and Kilmaine, who was both a field marshal and a diplomat.

On both landings these English soldiers and politicians are flanked by two German princes: one of the church and the other very much a man of the world, one Catholic and the other Protestant. On the upper landing the visitor may see the portrait of a youthful Habsburg prince, the Bishop Leopold of Passau, who was in effect the founder of the University of Passau. What he started as a seminary in 1611 quickly gained widespread acclaim. His decision to entrust the Jesuits with the running of the academy sealed its reputation. Four hundred years on, the University has not ceased to draw students from far and wide.

On the lower landing the visitor is scrutinized by Duke Johann Friedrich of Braunschweig-Lüneburg, a mighty seventeenth-century prince. He forms a tenuous link with his Hanoverian relations on the English throne, whose portraits dominate the gallery leading to the main reception rooms. The English Hanoverians all have their common ancestors in the Dukes of Braunschweig-Lüneburg.

Three early 18th-century portraits by Godfrey Kneller (1648–1723) of members of the Kit-Cat Club.

A glimpse of eighteenth-century English history can be caught on the way up to the reception rooms on the first floor. Amongst the pictures that flank the flight of stairs there are three portraits of members of London's "Kit-Cat Club", founded in 1700 by influential Whig patriots to ensure a Protestant succession at the end of William III's reign. The club took its name from the pastry cook Christopher Cat, in whose public house the group initially held their meetings. As the legend has it, it was not only the intellectual pleasure of skilled debate which drew the men to Mr. Cat's back rooms, but also his famous mutton pie.[1]

One of the club's members was the portrait painter Sir Godfrey Kneller. German born and bred, he had come to London in 1674, aged 28, and soon become one of the most acclaimed portrait painters. The scale and efficiency of his workshop in many ways anticipated the twentieth-century assembly line. Not only did his workshop employ individual assistants assigned to paint wigs, cloth,

The dukes' hereditary lands became realigned as much by strings of successions as by the gains and losses of martial policy and the vagaries of fortune on the battlefield, resulting in the formation of a number of independent branches of the family. One of these branches was that of the Dukes of Lüneburg-Celle, who subsequently took on the name of Hanover—the name by which the later Electors and Kings of Hanover were known.

These links between England and the Brunswicks—Braunschweigs—were far from being the first. Among the earlier connections was that of Henry the Lion (1129–95), Duke of Saxony and Bavaria, of the House of Welf (the Braunschweig / Hanover's family name), who had taken as his second wife Matilda (1156–89), daughter of the Plantagenet Henry II of England. The link which bore the greatest consequences, however, came about in 1714. Neither Mary II, who was daughter of the last Stuart king, Charles II, and became joint sovereign with her husband William III of the House of Orange, nor her sister, Anne, who became queen after her, left any heirs. There was their Catholic half-brother James's claim, but he was barred from the throne by the 1701 Act of Settlement. This parliamentary act regulated the succession of the Electress Sophia of Hanover and her Protestant descendants, bypassing not only a number of Catholics in the line of succession but also a possible, if disputable, claim from the House of Orange. Sophia was the granddaughter of James I and therefore a cousin of the two late Stuart queens. Her father was Frederick V, Elector Palatine of the Rhine and King of Bohemia, her mother Elizabeth Stuart, sister of Charles I. Frederick and Elizabeth had reigned in Prague for only a few winter months of 1619, at the onset of the Thirty Years' War. Defeated in the battle at the White Hill by the imperial army under Tilly, Frederick's short reign came to an end. He was called the "Winter King" in derision, but this byname secured his legacy in the history books. Their daughter Sophie married Ernst

August, Elector of Hanover. Sophie died in June 1714, Queen Anne in August that same year and so the succession fell to Sophie's eldest son George, who became King George I of Great Britain and Ireland, while still retaining his electorate of Hanover.

The subsequent dynastic separation of the two countries came about in 1837 with the death of William IV. His niece Victoria succeeded him in Britain and Ireland, whereas in Hanover Salic law barred her as a woman from the throne. The nearest man in line, William's younger brother Ernest Augustus, Duke of Cumberland, became King of Hanover instead.

The portraits of the English kings of the House of Hanover are grouped together on the landing, and the juxtaposition of three portraits in particular is of especial interest. They show George III at three stages of his life: in 1761, 1783 and around 1810. The viewing begins with the latest in this series, a small double portrait of quiet and intimate air. It originates from the workshop of Johann Zoffany and shows the elderly and suffering King, battered by his illnesses, together with his wife Queen Charlotte in the kind of private and homely setting they so cherished. Incidentally, Zoffany, too, was of German descent. Born 1733 in Frankfurt as Johann Edler von Zoffany, he came to England in 1776 where he became an acclaimed portrait painter and remained so right up to his death in 1810. The two other likenesses are large state portraits, and show a younger King. On either side of the large double doors leading into the reception rooms hang the two impressive coronation portraits of the King and his Queen, Charlotte, Princess of Mecklenburg-Strelitz, by Alan Ramsay. This George was of the fourth generation of British Hanoverians (he was the grandson of George II; his father, Frederick Prince of Wales, had predeceased him) and he felt exclusively British, unlike his grandfather and great grandfather, who had felt more at ease with the continental way of life and kept their German ties.

Coronation portraits of George III, and his wife, Queen Charlotte, by Alan Ramsay, 1761/62. Below, a pair of German Directoire benches from the late 18th century.

The portrait shows the proud young King at the outset of his reign, ready to take on parliament, which indeed he did. By 1761 he had forced the omnipotent and popular William Pitt out of office and one year later he had finally broken the Whig parliamentary majority, which ensured an almost unchallenged sway for the King's own conservative views. With fierce determination he wrestled back most of the constitutional powers which his two predecessors had let slip. As for his early foreign policy, he exercised his new strength and influence to end the Seven Years' War. It was during his reign that England rose to become the greatest colonial power of the world while her economy at home was undergoing fundamental changes through the industrial revolution. Yet despite these national achievements he never in his life gained personal popularity.

The portraits of King George and Queen Charlotte may be deemed something of a discovery, since for generations the paintings were believed lost. Two letters by Ramsay, still preserved today, give testimony to his Sovereign's commission. The first is dated 19th December 1761, directed to Lord Bute, the second from 10th January 1766 to the Lord Chamberlain, 3rd Duke of Portland.[2] In the letters the artist writes that he was commissioned to paint *two* portraits of George III: "a whole length picture of him for Hanover … dressed in coronation robes" only shortly after the coronation in 1761. With reference to the state portrait of the young Queen he writes in the second letter: "Soon after Her Majesty's arrival, she likewise did me the honour to sit to me; and these two pictures in the coronation robes are the originals from which all the copies ordered by the Lord Chamberlain are painted."

In this letter mention is likewise made of "… the pictures of the King intended for St James's and the full-length for Hanover …", both of which he was working on in December 1761. It was always known that there had been two identical sets of

26

coronation portraits by Ramsay's own hand. One set was known to be in the Royal Collection at Windsor Castle, while the whereabouts of the other remained unknown. It came as a pleasant surprise when, among the loans the Prince of Hanover made to the London embassy in 1992, these two paintings emerged from the packing cases. Their provenance, together with Ramsay's own testimony prove without a doubt that these are not any of the numerous studio copies of this popular subject, but genuinely Ramsay's first versions.

Below the coronation portraits is a pair of especially beautiful Directoire upholstered benches, dating from the late eighteenth century.

The third of the George III likenesses, again a state portrait, shows a portly man in his mid forties: his face reddened, his bearing heavy, his expression bespeaking a man of few illusions. Apart from ongoing interior struggles and worries, it was the time of England's war with the American colonies, a war which eventually led to America's independence.

When Alan Ramsay painted this portrait he had already been "His Majesty's Principal Painter in Ordinary" for some years.

The row of state portraits is rounded off by George II, George III's grandfather. Probably by Enoch Seemann, or at any rate from his studio, it was painted in 1730, shortly after the King's accession to the throne.

The English-Hanoverian theme on the landing is completed by a long-case clock from the famous and innovative Vulliamy clockmaker's workshop in London. By tracing its registration number (327) in the Royal archives it has been identified as a commission from the Duke of Cumberland, delivered to him on April 7th, 1801 for the sum of ten pounds and two shillings. Meticulous book-keeping records gain us even further insight into the Duke's expenditure: five pounds five shillings was the price of the clock mechanism, four pounds ten shillings for the case and seven shillings for the patent lock.[3]

When the Duke of Cumberland returned to Hanover upon Queen Victoria's accession to the throne in 1837, this clock was among the memorabilia he took back with him. In 1992 this venerable piece was sent back as a loan from the House of Hanover, to add to the display of objects betokening a rather personal relationship between England and Germany in the eighteenth and early nineteenth centuries.

Above the first-floor gallery hangs the largest of the embassy's Flemish tapestries. It is from the manufactory of J. de Vos of Brussels, made in the sixteenth century. The subject is from Greek mythology and shows Thetis, the sea nymph, bathing her son Achilles in the River Styx, a river of the underworld. This bath would have protected her son from any mortal danger had she not overlooked the heel by which she held him. Covered by her hand the "Achilles' heel" remained dry and became his only fatal weakness, which Paris, helped by the god Apollo, exploited to deadly effect in the battle of Troy.

Staircase with state portrait of George III by Alan Ramsay, 1783, and state portrait of George II, attributed to Enoch Seemann, 1730 (opposite).

An English long-case clock from the Vulliamy workshop, made in London for the Duke of Cumberland in 1801.

FIRST RECEPTION ROOM (ANTEROOM)

Adjoining the landing area begins the series of reception rooms, their splendour enhanced by a vivid colour scheme in the taste of the mid-nineteenth century. For the first, the anteroom, a pale terracotta colour was chosen for the walls, the frieze ornaments picked out in a black glaze.

The walls set a neo-classical tone, which is picked up by some of the furniture such as an exceptional north German Biedermeier *secrétaire* made of walnut with brass embellishments. Its tall front is made up of two bottom drawers and a fall-front top, flanked by full-size columns on fire-gilt mounts. Its raised top with a convex central door is also set in a column and pediment frame, flanked by two concave doors.

Above the fireplace as a central eye-catcher hangs a huge early nineteenth-century mirror, possibly German. The mahogany panel of 2.60 metres (c. 8 ft. 6 in.) in height is three-quarters covered by mirror glass. The bold, gilded ribboned laurel wreath beneath the flat gable is somewhat in contrast to the rather more filigree ornaments of Greek and Egyptian adaptations. It was a fashion which swept all over Europe at the turn of the eighteenth century,

Wall and frieze detail in anteroom.

A Biedermeier secrétaire, north German, from around 1820.

A charming mid 18th-century four-leaf screen with the Nymphenburg Palace in Munich, summer palace of the Electors of Bavaria.

not least after Napoleon's Egyptian campaign.

On the chimneypiece stands a replica of Johann Gottfried Schadow's statue of the Princesses Luise and Friederike of Mecklenburg-Strelitz (of the same family as Queen Charlotte, wife of George III) from 1792 to 1794. This double portrait, originally life size and in marble, is well known and close to the heart of many Germans. Contemporary scale models were cast in their thousands by the Königliche Porzellan-Manufaktur [Royal Porcelain Manufactory] of Berlin. Princess Luise was the legendary wife of the well-meaning though weak-willed Prussian king Friedrich-Wilhelm III. Their life was marked by an almost bourgeois domestic happiness amid the turmoil of the Napoleonic wars. They were their people's role model for a harmonious and peaceful marital partnership, and Luise was idolized for her brave encounter with Napoleon in Tilsit where she sought to spare her country from being drawn into war. Her untimely death in 1810 turned admiration for her into almost religious worship. Her sister Friederike, who wed Friedrich Wilhelm's younger brother Friedrich, had a less fulfilled married life. After having been widowed twice she took as her third husband none

other than Ernest Augustus, Duke of Cumberland, and in 1837 became Queen of Hanover.

To the right of the fireplace stands a lovely, sturdy Baroque chest of drawers of veneered walnut and walnut root. It has four drawers and rests on lathe-turned feet. The curved and angular band inlays point to a mid eighteenth-century south German origin. Above it hangs an oil painting by Bernardo Bellotto (1720–80) who, like his uncle Giovanni Antonio Canal, signed himself as "Canaletto". It shows a lively scene by one of Venice's less glamorous canals. On either side of the chest of drawers are two surprising chairs, their curves and shapes quite in the Baroque style of the 1720s and 30s, but their backs each adorned with an unusually wide and flat carved shell motif. Chairs of that description would originally have been Portuguese; in this case it is most probably a German adaptation.

The furniture in this room is completed with a French suite of six armchairs and a *canapé* in the style of Louis XVI, which dates, however, from a period of a late nineteenth-century revival of this style, known as *deuxième rococo*. Until not too long ago spurned as imitations, they are now deemed valuable pieces in their own right, particularly when their original upholstery has been preserved, as is the case here.

Among the rest of the furniture, and treasured more for its charm than for artistic value, is the screen in the left hand corner. Its four leaves are covered with a canvas depicting the west elevation, gardens and canal of the Schloss Nymphenburg, the palatial summer residence of the Wittelsbach Electors of Bavaria, situated in what were then rural hunting grounds outside Munich. It was built under the Elector Max II Emanuel in the late seventeenth and early eighteenth century, and its exterior has remained pretty much unchanged. The illustrious Elector was barely able to catch an occasional glimpse of his palace as much of his life was spent either on the battlefield or in exile. These misfortunes resulted from his siding with the losing French troops in the War of the Spanish Succession. The most momentous of these battles was that of Höchstadt, or, as it is known in English history books, the Battle of Blenheim, where fortune smiled on the Habsburg-English coalition under Marlborough. As well as fame and other honours, this battle brought the Duke of Marlborough the imperial gift of the Bavarian town of Mindelheim, with all its tax revenues.

An Italian landscape by Jakob Philipp Hackert (1773–1807) rounds off the classical note of this room. Hackert belonged to the first generation of the circle of the so-called "German Romans", a group of German painters who had gathered in Rome in the first half of the nineteenth century and shared an admiration for Italian painting, especially from the sixteenth century. We have already met two younger generation painters of this circle in the Inner Hall downstairs: Ainmiller and Schnorr von Carolsfeld. The older Hackert is still caught up in the classical ideals. His *Southern Landscape with Villa by a Lake* owes much to the study of classic heroic Italian landscape painting in Rome and also Naples, though softened by the late eighteenth-century rococo touch. In the foreground a rococo shepherdess tends her sheep against a classical backdrop of a tempietto, which closely resembles Palladio's Villa Pisani in

Still Life with Vases by Alexey von Jawlensky, 1930.

Montagnana; albeit with the addition of an enormous flight of stairs leading down to the lake.

Admittedly, there is not much modern art to speak of in the embassy. However, one still life by the Russian-born artist Alexey von Jawlensky (1864–1941) is worthy of mention. In 1896 he forsook his career as an officer, left his middle-class family and moved to Munich to study painting, where he met Kandinsky. There ensued a fruitful collaboration. Other like-minded artists, such as Gabriele Münther, Marianne von Werefkin, Paul Klee, Alfred Kubin and August Macke, inspired the two Russian expatriates to found the "Neue Münchner Künstlervereinigung" in 1909, which later led to the formation of a new group "Der Blaue Reiter", named after Kandinsky's painting *The Blue Rider*. At the beginning of World War I Jawlensky went into exile and spent the following years in Switzerland. He returned to Germany in 1921 and died in Wiesbaden in 1941.

Below the painting stands a small concave, canted chest of drawers made of burr walnut with fruitwood and ash marquetry on scrolled acanthus feet; it is north German or Dutch from around 1740.

YELLOW DRAWING ROOM

Yellow drawing room (previous spread).

Wide openings lead to the principal drawing room, which has been painted a soft yellow, the frieze picked out in cream and apricot, creating an overall warm and light effect in this west-facing room. A suite of open-armed chairs and sofas invites visitors to a more intimate gathering, equally allowing the eye to wander right and left to enjoy the enfilade of the three large reception rooms. The seating furniture comprises two six-legged sofas covered in stripy cream-yellow silk, both with padded, rectangular backs and arms of the same height. Seven chairs, six with and one without armrests, as well as a footstool, complete the set. Their wooden frames are carved and painted in white and gold. Even though this set is much akin to French Louis XVI furniture, the angular, high side-rests and the splayed back legs indicate its English origin. This is what was described in its day as Whig family furniture and dates from around 1780 to 1790, when French period furniture was very much in vogue.

The outer sofa is backed by a fiddleback mahogany Regency sofa table of high quality. It has rounded rectangular twin flap-tops, cross-banded with tulipwood. Two cedar-lined drawers are inserted into the frieze and the scrolled legs are joined by a stretcher.

Above the suite of chairs hangs a large Flemish, sixteenth-century Gobelin, of similar subdued hues. Its theme would have made a learned conversation piece and displayed the philosophical knowledge of its commissioning patron. It is most probably missing its pendant. What we see here are only two of the four Cardinal Virtues. All in all there are seven canonical virtues, made up of the three Theological Virtues: Faith (*Fides*), Hope (*Spes*) and Charity (*Caritas*), and the four Cardinal Virtues: Prudence (*Prudentia*), Temperance (*Temperantia*), Fortitude (*Fortitudo*) and Justice (*Justitia*). For this particular Gobelin two of the virtues—*Fides* and *Temperantia*—were chosen. They are personified

along the border, together with their attributes. Central to the tapestry is a garden scene reminiscent of the Garden of Eden, where Faith and Temperance are shown in three different tableaux, exercising their virtues for the edification of the beholder.

Next to it on the short wall is perhaps the most eye-catching of the paintings in this room: *Lady in Red Velvet* by François Gérard, court portrait painter under both Napoleon and Louis XVIII. It is uncertain whether it depicts Hortense Beauharnais, daughter of the Empress Josephine, who married Napoleon's younger brother Louis and was Queen of Holland for a while, or whether it is Napoleon's second wife Marie-Louise, the Habsburg Archduchess who was forced into this marriage in the hope of pacifying the angry Corsican.

The short wall next to this has a very different portrait as its focal point: The *Portrait of a Girl* by Wilhelm von Kaulbach (1805–74). The sitter is not the self-conscious lady of the world but a shy young girl, slightly ill at ease, not elegant but proper for a young girl at home, with her hair loose, wearing a white blouse and pink skirt. Alongside the younger artist Franz von Lenbach, Kaulbach was a leading figure in the Munich art world of the nineteenth century. Both were society portrait painters, and resided in princely palaces in Munich. Today the palaces have become museums and home to some of Munich's best art collections.

Below the portrait we find a chest of drawers of probably German, or possibly Dutch origin from the mid eighteenth century. Inlaid with walnut and burr maple cross bands, its two long drawers bow gracefully outwards. It stands high on cabriole legs with hoofed feet. Its marble top is a later replacement of the original wooden one.

Between the windows stand a pair of mid eighteenth-century card tables of German or French origin. Above on the left is a painting by Adrianus

François Gérard:
Lady in Red
Velvet.

Mountain Landscape with Hunters. Adrianus Koekkoek, mid 19th century.

Koekkoek (1807–70), *Mountain Landscape with Hunters*. The Dutch Koekkoek family produced a number of painters from the eighteenth to the twentieth century; of whom Adrianus was the most popular.

The corresponding painting between the next windows will bring smiles of recognition and recollection to almost every onlooker: a Venetian capriccio by Giovanni Antonio Canal (1697–1768), better known as Canaletto. He was the uncle of

Bernardo Bellotto already mentioned; both having worked under the "Canaletto" signature. This capriccio consists of an array of palaces and bridges crammed along an imaginary Venetian Canal. The buildings are all by Andrea Palladio; some real, others never got beyond the blueprint stage. Canaletto brought them together for his vision of an ideal town. From Vicenza he took the Basilica (right) and the Palazzo Chiericati (left), and the bridge is based on drawings which Palladio

submitted for a contest to design the Rialto Bridge. Although the Signoria rejected his plans, his drawings were to become the epitome of the classical bridge and were copied and adapted all over the world, particularly in eighteenth-century English parks, such as Wilton House, Stowe or Prior Park.

The wide opening towards the dining room is framed by a pair of delicate marquetry commodes of Italian origin, from the circle of Giuseppe Maggiolini. They date from the turn of the eighteenth century. Under the richly ornamented frieze drawer there are two quarter veneered drawers inlaid with a medallion bearing a Ganymede motif referring to the myth of the handsome youth being carried off by Zeus disguised as an eagle. Identical medallions appear again on the sides and tops of the commodes.

If the commodes are a pair, so too are the two sets of paintings above them: The larger ones arc by the German Johann Elias Riedinger (1698–1767), who

Capriccio of
Venetian Palaces
by Canaletto
(Giovanni
Antonio Canal),
mid 18th century.

Stag Hunt. Mid 18th-century oil painting by Johann Elias Riedinger.

A corner in the yellow drawing room with a Maggiolini commode, south German mirror, late 18th century, and paintings by Riedinger (1st half 18th century) and Teniers (mid 17th century)

was best known for his wildlife, animal and hunting scenes which circulated in vast editions of prints from his own workshop. His oil paintings, such as *Stag Hunt* (left) and *Boar Hunt* (right) are quite rare and a lucky find. The tempestuous landscape is really only a stage dressing to show men, hounds and horses in every form of contortion and agitation. Both paintings follow the same narrative scheme: in the background, like a small-scale inset, the events preceding the hunt are depicted whereas in the foreground on larger scale the same figures and animals are shown in the turmoil of the triumphant climax.

Below the Riedingers are two small genre paintings of the mid seventeenth century of the circle of the Flemish painter David Teniers.

ROOM LEADING TO DINING ROOM

Left from the yellow room the enfilade proceeds into the large L-shaped dining room. Its walls sport a dark terracotta, with the frieze picked out in darker bluish-green and cream. The Corinthian pillars dividing the two spaces of the "L" have been given a marbled paint effect, its tone corresponding with that of the frieze, yet richer and with a hint of brown. In this room most of the embassy's tapestries are grouped together. Their tawny colours go well with the warm subtleties of the polished wooden furniture and larger scale paintings, blending the pieces into a homogenous ensemble that is Baroque in feel, if not necessarily in style.

The first of the Gobelins to catch the eye is of Flemish origin and dates from the late sixteenth century. It is richly interwoven with gold threads, suggesting that the commission came from a noble and wealthy patron. The religious theme does not necessarily suggest an ecclesiastical patron: merchants might sometimes have been as deeply religious as clergymen were sometimes worldly! The tapestry shows three scenes from the exemplary life of the charitable St. Matilda, an early tenth-century noblewoman and the wife of the Duke of Saxony, who later became the Holy Roman Emperor Henry I. They were the parents of the Emperor Otto I and thus progenitors of the line of the Ottonian kings. Matilda was canonized soon after her death, which explains the belief of subsequent generations of Ottonians that they were blessed and chosen by God.

The mahogany dresser below is a beautiful example of Regency cabinet-making. The outline of the tabletop's slight curve is traced by delicate, threadlike inlay. The centre of the fluted frieze below is emphasized by an inlaid plate motif of a shallow bowl filled with vine leaves and grapes. The tapering legs are of corresponding subtle delicacy. Although very English in appearance, there are characteristics which might well bespeak an American origin.

The tapering octagonal cellaret underneath is English from the mid nineteenth century and therefore slightly younger than the dresser. It holds up to eight bottles for cooling—surely an important piece of furniture for any hospitable patrician! On the dresser, and appropriately close to the saintly tapestry, stands a Gothic sandstone angel from north Germany.

More wordly are the two paintings on the adjacent wall: from the early eighteenth century dates a cheerful *Funfair with Booth* by the Flemish painter Pieter Angillis, and above it hangs *Palace Ruins* by the Italian Giovanni Pannini (1692–1765), who was famous for his architectural paintings. Even though the ruinous theme has been set in a shady moonlit night, the subject is lent a certain gaiety by the putti amid garlands of flowers, who

Detail of Corinthian pillars, wall and frieze of dining room.

Section of the dining room with Flemish Gobelin, English dresser and paintings by Giovanni Pannini and Pieter Angillis (opposite).

Funfair with Booth by Pieter Angillis. Flemish, early 18th century.

seem to flirt with these symbols of transience in a very Baroque fashion.

Complementing these two paintings on the other side of the room we see Verbruggen's *Still Life with Flowers* hanging above a Baroque table of about 1720–30 from southern Germany. Its top is inlaid with foliage and scrolls and the same design is repeated, this time three-dimensionally in the carving on the cabriole legs. Similar pieces were made for the castle of Pommersfelden, built from

1711 onwards for Lothar Franz von Schönborn, Bishop of Bamberg and Elector of Mainz.

The painting of the Battle of Blenheim between the windows merits further scrutiny. It is a copy of the much larger eighteenth-century original in Turin. At one time this copy was thought to have been commissioned by the Prussian King Frederick I to commemorate Prussia's role in the War of the Spanish Succession. We now know that it was ordered much later by King William of Prussia (who

was to become the first German Emperor William I) at some time before 1870. As a means of propaganda Prussian troops were introduced into this display of the victorious Habsburg-English alliance, even though the Prussians, albeit allies, had not taken part in this particular battle of 1704. The Prussian royal family showed particular interest in this battle because the Emperor in Vienna had been desperate for allies to back up his claim to the Spanish throne in the wars of 1701 to 1714. His opponent was the

King of France, who was not to be underestimated as an adversary. When the Prussian Elector Frederick III brought his army under the Emperor's flags, the Emperor in turn agreed not to oppose the crowning of the Elector as "King in Prussia" in Königsberg. This was a clever move and diplomatic masterpiece on both sides. The Emperor was in pressing need for troops and therefore susceptible to blackmail. Prussia was in possession of what was probably the most efficient army in Europe—and

The Battle of Blenheim, commissioned around 1870 by King William of Prussia, later Emperor William I. A copy of the larger 18th-century original.

that was worth a high price. In spite of all that the Emperor did not entertain the idea of there being yet another king on the territory of his Holy Roman Empire. The answer to this dilemma was soon found by using Prussia's complex constitutional position: the Prussian territories consisted, among others, of the electorate of Brandenburg (which was part of the Habsburg realm) and the hereditary duchy of Prussia with its capital Königsberg, which was outside the Habsburg territory. In accepting the style of King "in" Prussia both men had it their way; one was raised to king, whereas the other did not lose face by investing this new king himself. So it is not by chance that some 160 years later the battle

was again pulled out of the attics of history. On the eve of King William's elevation to German Emperor it was considered the right moment to re-polish the story which had played such a crucial role in his ancestor King Frederick's I's creation: this was the inspiration behind the copy—adjusted slightly with the addition of Prussian troops.

For the royal line of succession to the English throne this battle was no less important. George Louis, Elector of Hanover, had already fought with determined courage in the wars of his uncle William III of the House of Orange, husband of Queen Mary II. Later he had sent a welcome reinforcement of Hanoverians to fight under Marlborough at

Blenheim. With prudent persistence he attached himself closely to the Whigs and to Marlborough, refusing Tory offers of an independent command. In return for his fidelity he received a guarantee by the Dutch ensuring his succession to England in the Barrier Treaty of 1709.[4] With the death of Queen Anne, sister of Mary, both of whom had left no heirs, he became George I King of Great Britain and Ireland.

The painting between the following windows is in peaceful contrast to battle and high politics. Adolf Friedrich Harper's *Heroic Landscape* depicts the romanticized rustic life of hermits and shepherds amongst picturesque ruins. Harper lived in Rome in the 1750s, and was acquainted with the German intellectual circle there. One of these intellectuals was Johann Joachim Winckelmann. However, Harper's artistic education and inspiration came mainly from an English group in Rome, especially from Richard Wilson.

Among the chests of drawers the most notable piece is a bow-fronted walnut chest, made either in Saxony or in Poland in the late eighteenth century.

The remarkable design of its brass fittings with mascarons and electoral caps suggests that it probably came from the Elector of Saxony's household. At that time the heirs of the House of Wettin held their original electorate of Saxony and were also elected Kings of Poland. It is decorated with linear fruitwood inlays, has square banded corners and toupee feet.

Without doubt the focal point of this room is an English gilt overmantel mirror hanging above the fireplace, duplicating the whole long enfilade. The mirrored borders are divided by a band of bead-and-reel. On top is a separate oval mirror, supported by two phoenixes. The Pompeiian motifs as well as the thin, delicate ornamentation date the mirror to the late nineteenth century. Though it may be a slightly later copy of an Adam one, it is nevertheless strikingly attractive.

On either side of the mirror two large genre scenes by Giuseppe Gambarini, dating from the early eighteenth century, one with a shepherd motif, the other a group of arcadian card players.

An impressive late 18th-century chest of drawers, made of walnut. Probably from the household of the Elector of Saxony.

CENTRAL DINING ROOM

Dining room with maiolica plates and Gobelins (previous spread).

A turn to the left through the wide, pillar-framed opening reveals the heart of the dining room. The visitor's attention is immediately drawn to the glamorous display of a George II gilded mirror surrounded by a collection of seven colourful Italian maiolica plates above the fireplace. Such plates are very rare and it is rarer still to find so many in one group. They are most certainly among the more outstanding works of art in the embassy. From the second half of the sixteenth century, they originate from the many little workshops that flourished in northern Italy, especially in Venice, Urbino and Padua. Not unusually for the time, they nearly all depict religious subjects, mainly from the Old Testament. The artisans did not invent the motifs, but copied them from popular contemporary woodcuts and prints. The scenes of *Saul and David* and *David and Ahimelech* were taken from a woodcut by Bernard Salomon, whereas *Abraham and the Three Angels* takes G. de Roville's woodcut as a model. Further scenes are *Saul's Conversion*, *The Destruction of the Brazen Serpent* and *Samuel Slays the King of the Amalekites*. As well as legends and biblical themes, Greek mythology was also a major source of artistic inspiration at the time. One illustration shows *Tiresias*, the blind seer who told Odysseus the future when he visited the underworld.

The English gilded George II mirror lends even more sparkle to this display.

What dominates every dining room is, of course, the dining table, here laid with onion pattern china, probably Meissen's most widely known design, and with Meissen figurines from the *commedia dell'arte*. Also worth mentioning are the three dressers in this room. To the sides of the fireplace are two serpentine front sideboards of mahogany, dating from the reigns of George II and George III. Opposite stands the most venerable of the three, an English low dresser of elm and oak from the late seventeenth century. It has a moulded rectangular top above a row of geometrically panelled drawers, and rests on turned baluster legs.

Italian maiolica plate, second half of 16th century: Samuel Slays the King of the Amalekites.

George II gilded mirror surrounded by seven Italian maiolica plates, second half of 16th century (far right).

To the right and to the left of the fireplace hang two more tapestries of the embassy's noteworthy collection; both of distinctly different character and purpose. The one on the left dates from the second half of the sixteenth century. Neither legend nor bible nor mythology, this is a wall news-sheet; a piece of political propaganda. It shows the victorious Emperor Charles V and the defeated Elector Johann Friedrich of Saxony after the events of the Battle of Mühlberg in 1547, when the emperor routed the troops of the Schmalkaldischer Bund— the Smalkaldic League—by which he broke up the Protestant Union. The wall hanging was made only shortly afterwards, with coarse wool to enable faster progress. It is a run-of-the-mill product with little regard for artistic composition, designed for a non-reading or writing audience. Although the bold colouring and the blunt didacticism may appear amusing to us, it was then a most effective means of indoctrination, which avoided any possible misunderstanding. The message was taken seriously and its effectiveness was reinforced by its constant presence.

The Gobelin on the right hand side could not be more different. It was executed at about the same time, though woven more delicately and of richer material, and it has a more everlasting theme— although defining what that might be is a bit of a puzzle. The tapestry shows signs of having been trimmed in earlier times so that it does not show the entire picture. This in itself is not unusual since these wall-hangings were moved around to decorate and warm a room, and were regarded more as a useful piece of equipment than a sacred work of art. What we now see in the centre is a regal figure, enthroned upon a triumphal, wheeled platform in an Egyptian-like pose. His face is in sharp profile, his body turned towards us. The sphinx reinforces the Egyptian theme. A caravan of camels before a palm tree grove forms the backdrop, and a monkey features in the foreground on the left. Palm branches are held by the monarch and by five

assisting female figures surrounding the platform. The palms here could be interpreted as Christian emblems. The main figure may well be King Solomon, who had married the daughter of Pharaoh, thereby securing a good relationship between the two powers during his reign. The palm leaves variously symbolize martyrdom, victory, ascent, rebirth and (Christian) immortality. This may be one of the rare cases of Solomon iconography where his succession to King David is compared to Christ's triumphal palm-strewn entrance into Jerusalem, thereby emphasizing the continuity between the Old and New Testaments. Palm leaves were also used to decorate Solomon's temple in Jerusalem.[5] The main figure is clearly a man of wealth and splendour, lending credence to the assumption that this might indeed be Solomon. Furthermore, the five obviously high-ranking women by his side might allude to Solomon's polygamy, which is mentioned in the 1st Book of Kings, 11, 4. Even if Solomon's identity cannot be confirmed with absolute certainty, the probability is high.

A further Gobelin adorns the wall opposite and complements the furnishings. This one is from the early eighteenth century—rather recent compared with the other tapestries in the embassy's collection. In dark greens and browns it shows floral and feral motifs. These colours are picked up in the six-leaved Japanese lacquer screen standing nearby, creating a pleasing harmony between two objects from such different cultures.

The narrow wall between the east windows ends with a northern German gilded mahogany mirror from the middle of the eighteenth century, with an arched cresting and a gilt fruit basket for its central motif.

A 16th-century Gobelin
in the dining room,
probably showing King
Solomon.

MUSIC ROOM

At the opposite end of the enfilade of state rooms is the music room. Unlike the others its plasterwork is of rococo derivation and has therefore been given an appropriate pale blue, grey and cream wall finish. This matches the overall cream, white and ivory upholstery of the central group of easy chairs and *canapé* in the style of Louis XVI, and goes equally well with the pretty Aubusson carpet. Its delicate and detailed pattern of flowers, ribbons, bouquets and medallions, on a raspberry red and turquoise background, dates it to the time of Louis-Philippe, around 1830. This arrangement of seating furniture also features a small occasional table with a plain circular top above a simple frieze inlaid with vertical beech and walnut stripes. It is supported by four thin, square tapering legs; a fairly typical German style at the turn of the eighteenth century.

In front of the *canapé* there are two more of the *deuxième rococo* armchairs from the Anteroom set next to a round Louis XVI *guéridon* table with marble top and brass fixings from the later eighteenth century.

The origin of the suite of four beechwood chairs, two of them with, two without armrests, has been much disputed. Their style is north German rococo. There are, however, certain elements which point to English cabinet-making: the way the slender, fluted and tapering legs are set, the broad padded seats and backs may even suggest some link to the cabinet-maker John Linnell.

If one were to pick one piece of furniture from this room it would have to be the tabernacle *secrétaire* of the middle of the eighteenth century. The serpentine base consists of three drawers followed by a sloping top, which reveals little drawers and pigeonholes. It is surmounted by a domed cabinet top with a central door, framed on either side by rows of five drawers each. Made of walnut and inlaid with burr walnut, the cabinet still has its original brass mountings. It is a

View into the music room.

typical piece of furniture from the Brunswick area.

The Hanoverian clock collection is represented by another piece: an English bracket clock with a tortoiseshell case, which is richly inlaid and mounted with brass. Its face and movement comes from Vulliamy's London workshop. Since it was part of the loan from the Prince of Hanover to the London embassy, it must have been made for the Court, either for George III or George IV. During that time a large number of clocks in the Royal Household underwent a general overhaul, chiefly to replace the ageing movements by modern, more reliable ones from the reputable Vulliamy workshops. This accounts for the frequency with which nineteenth-century clock mechanisms are found in eighteenth-century clocks, as is the case here.

A late Baroque bracket clock of tortoiseshell, with brass and gilt mounts and inlays.

Of the two chests of drawers on either side of the fireplace, the chest with three drawers on the right rests on claw-and-ball feet. Its marquetry is in the Boulle style, but is of wood rather than metal. This piece of furniture is from mid eighteenth-century western Germany, possibly from cabinet-makers of the town of the episcopal court of Mainz, then one of the leading furniture-making centres. The second commode is a rather amusing German provincial marquetry chest with a pronounced double bow front on sturdy bun feet, and dates from the first half of the eighteenth century. On display are two large porcelain groups of men and horses from the Bavarian Nymphenburg manufactory; part of the relatively modest china collection of the embassy.

Two paintings complete the back wall: *Still Life with Prey* by Jacob Andries Breschey with a greyhound eyeing the trophies of the day's hunting, and *Still Life with Thistles, Bird and Butterfly* by Caspar Hirschley.

One other painting is especially noteworthy, the enchanting *Princess in White* painted by Anna Fries (1827–1901). She was an acclaimed artist and had a remarkable career for a woman of her day. Dutch by birth, she had travelled widely. Among many commissions were those she did as court portraitist in the Netherlands; she was an honorary member of the Florentine Accademia di Belle Arti and also the head of the "Art Academy for Ladies" in Florence. The *Princess* is typical of its genre; a society portrait of around 1860–70, when painters such as Winterhalter were at the zenith of their careers.

A pair of narrow Italian giltwood mirrors, with sectional mirror frames dating to the second third of the eighteenth century, completes the furnishing of this room.

THE AMBASSADOR'S OFFICE

The furniture in the Ambassador's office is of course primarily suited to the room's functional use. The principal item, naturally, is the desk; formerly belonging to Prince Lichnowsky. While it is by no means a valuable antique, it is certainly a sturdy and well-made piece of utility furniture from the late nineteenth century. When the embassy was re-opened in 1955, the Lichnowsky family made the desk available and since then it has served every one of the German ambassadors to the Court of St. James.

A few more items are of historical interest in this room, such as a portrait of the "Iron Chancellor" Otto von Bismarck by Franz von Lenbach from 1880. Lenbach lived from 1836 to 1904 and was one of the most sought after portrait artists of his time. His extravagantly opulent lifestyle attested to his popularity and success, and today his villa in Munich has been turned into a museum. The Lenbachhaus not only contains Lenbach's own works but is also known for its significant collection of Blauer Reiter and other early twentieth-century paintings.

The surprising sketch-like double portrait by the same artist portrays Döllinger and Gladstone, but whether these two ever actually sat together for the artist is unknown. It is certain, however, that Döllinger—a quarrelsome church politician and professor of theology from Munich who was also linked with the Oxford Tractarian Movement— kept up a lively correspondence with Gladstone about religious matters. Döllinger was eventually excommunicated by the Pope over the doctrine of papal infallibility. In protest the University of Oxford awarded him an honorary doctorate of Law—not of Theology, though.

There is a further reminder of German intellectual influence on British life—and indeed vice versa—in the shape of a plaster bust of Wilhelm von Humboldt; a great scholar and statesman, founder of Berlin University, and brother of the

Otto von Bismarck, painted in 1880 by Franz von Lenbach (1836–1904).

Döllinger and Gladstone, in an oil sketch by Franz von Lenbach, late 19th century.

explorer Alexander von Humboldt. Wilhelm served as Prussian Envoy to London from 1816 to 1819.

The remaining chairs belong to the set of German Baroque armchairs in the inner entrance.

Here the tour of the embassy comes to a preliminary end. There is another suite of three reception rooms on the ground floor, but they are less frequently used and await further refurbishment.

This is a young embassy, in the sense that it has not been able to build up its own collection of art over the generations. It is also different from what one might expect in that the embassy's collection of art and furniture is not exclusively of German origin. Instead it represents a variety of styles, historical periods, countries of origin; an appropriate echo, perhaps, not merely of Germany today, but also of her role in a wider Europe.

The Ambassador's office (opposite).

Notes
1. From *The London Encyclopedia*, Weinreb, Ben and Christopher Hibbert, London 1983.
2. *Catalogue of the Pictures Belonging to His Grace the Duke of Portland*, Goulding, R.W. and C.K. Adams, London, 1936, pp. 470–2.
3. From the Vulliamy records in the Public Record Office.
4. *The Encyclopedia Britannica*, 14th edition, London 1929, 10, 183 b.
5. Old Testament: I Kings 6:29–32, 35; 7:36; II Chronicles 3:5.

SELECT BIBLIOGRAPHY

Beal, Mary: *Works of Art, British Embassy Bonn*, London, 1990.

Biancheri, Boris: *The Italian Embassy in London,* 2nd edition, London, 1988.

Colvin, Howard: *A Biographical Dictionary of British Architects 1600–1840*, London, 1978.

Ferber, Elfriede: *Ullstein Möbelbuch,* Frankfurt, Berlin, Vienna, 1969.

Hill, Roland: *An Embassy in Belgrave Square*, London, 1991.

Hobhouse, Hermione: *Thomas Cubitt, Master Builder*, London 1995?

Metropole London: *Macht und Glanz einer Weltstadt*, Exhibition Catalogue, Villa Hügel, Essen, 1992.

Millar, Oliver: *The Later Georgian Pictures in the Collection of Her Majesty the Queen*, London, 1969.

Miller, Judith and Martin (editors): *The Antiques Directory - Furniture*, New York, 1988.

Sasse, Heinz Gunther: 100 Jahre Botschaft in London, *Aus der Geschichte der Deutschen Botschaft*, Bonn, 1963.

Service, Alastair: *The Architects of London and Their Buildings from 1066 to the Present Day*, London, 1979.

Smart, Alastair: *Alan Ramsay 1713–1784,* Exhibition Catalogue, Edinburgh and London, 1992.

Summerson, John: *Georgian London*, 5th edition. London, 1991.

Replica of Johann Gottfried Schadow's statue of the Princesses Luise and Friederike of Mecklenburg-Strelitz.

LENDERS TO THE EMBASSY

Bundesdepot, Bonn
Bayerische Staatsgemäldesammlungen, Munich
Deutsches Historisches Museum, Berlin
Germanisches Nationalmuseum, Nuremberg
Hamburger Kunsthalle, Hamburg
S.K.H. Prinz Ernst August von Hannover
Landesmuseum für Kunst- und Kulturgeschichte, Oldenburg
Museum Schnütgen, Cologne
Niedersächsisches Landesmuseum, Hanover
Schleswig-Holsteinisches Landesmuseum, Kiel
Städtische Galerie im Lenbachhaus, Munich
Stiftung Preussischer Kulturbesitz, Berlin
Württembergisches Landesmuseum, Stuttgart

ACKNOWLEDGEMENTS

We wish to extend our thanks to all who helped in the publication of this book, in particular:
Charles Cator
Jane Roberts
Hugh Roberts
Jo Wisdom
John Gaw

PHOTOGRAPHIC ACKNOWLEDGEMENTS

Fritz Graf von der Schulenburg 2, 15, 17, 18, top 19, bottom 19, 20, 21, 23, 24, 26–7, 29, 30–1, 31, 33, 34–5, 37, 39, 41, 42, 43, 44, 48–9, 51, 54–5, 56, 57, 59, 60

Marianne Majerus 28, 32, 38, 40, 45, 46, 47, 50, 53, 58

We should like to thank the following for making copyright photographs available:
Museum of London, London 6; **National Portrait Gallery**, London 9; **Fitzwilliam Museum**, Cambridge 12

INDEX

Page numbers for illustrations are shown in boldface type.